1-Hour Expert: Negotiating Your Job Offer™

Notice of rights

Trademarks

1-Hour Expert, 1-Hour Expert: Negotiating Your Job Offer, Master Vision Preparation (MVP), Master Vision Preparation (MVP) Worksheet, MVP Worksheet, Counterpart Analysis Plan (CAP), Counterpart Analysis Plan (CAP) Worksheet, CAP Worksheet, Strategy Formulation (SF) Worksheet, SF Worksheet.

Services for our readers

Colleges, business schools, corporate purchasing:
1-Hour Expert offers special discounts and supplemental materials for universities, business schools, and corporate training.
Contact us at: info@1-hourexpert.com

"This publication is designed to provide accurate and authoritative information in regard to the subject matter covered. It is sold with the understanding that the publisher and authors are not engaged in rendering legal, accounting, or other professional services. If legal advice or other expert assistance is required, seek the services of a competent professional."

—from a *Declaration of Principles*, jointly adopted by a committee of the American Bar Association and a committee of publishers

An Overview

What to expect from this Book

In four simple stages containing ten straightforward steps, this guide provides the complete roadmap needed to achieve your goals. It offers a comprehensive inventory of proven strategies that have already brought success to countless individuals. Designed specifically for time-constrained readers, this manual is the first to place this full range of techniques into a single concise document.

Our Process

Studies have found that learning and implementing negotiation skills are best accomplished through an interactive step-by-step process. The system you are about to explore has been honed to use the most effective and efficient tools available, allowing you to leverage your time to obtain the best results possible. To maximize the value you will extract, we will ask you in each step to complete some type of action. If there is a relevant key negotiation principle, we will explain it and show you how to apply it to your negotiations.

Figure 1:
You'll notice bullseye icons on each page. The highlighted ring indicates which stage of the process we are discussing.

VISUALIZE   ANALYZE   STRATEGIZE   IMPLEMENT

Steps 1 - 2   Steps 3 - 6   Steps 7 - 8   Steps 9 - 10

Stage One

Visualize Your Goal

An ancient proverb states that a journey of a thousand miles begins with a single step. In any negotiation, the first step toward your ideal job is always the establishment of a vision—the desired end you seek to reach.

Steps 1 and 2 are your opportunity to create and refine your vision. You will begin by determining the exact elements you desire, and then clarifying the level of importance you ascribe to each. In a short amount of time, you will reach a greater understanding of precisely what you want to achieve, which is the key to making it happen.

> **Note:** In Appendix 1, we provide a Master Vision Preparation (MVP) Worksheet to organize the information you'll provide in Steps 1 to 5. The MVP is designed to streamline your interests, goals and specific circumstances into a master vision statement, the guide for success in your negotiation process. Completing such a template forms the bedrock of the path to obtaining your ideal job. We recommend you look through the MVP template and other appendices at this point and work through each as it is discussed in the following steps.

STEP 1: CREATE YOUR VISION

First, build a list of the characteristics of your ideal job. The MVP in Appendix 1 provides a comprehensive list of key elements for convenience, but we encourage you to adapt it to your particular situation and consider which important items should be added to it. Some of the key questions to consider include:

▸ What position and role would you have?
▸ What responsibilities would you hold?

Visualize

- What type of career advancement opportunities and timeline do you desire?
- Would you have an office? Where would you be located? How would your personal work area look?
- Do you want to travel? If so, how often and to where?
- What hours would you work? What work/life balance and flexibility would you want?
- With what type of supervisor would you like to work?
- Do you want people working for you? With you?
- How much vacation would you like?
- What medical benefits do you desire?
- What kinds of perks are important to you? Company car? Cell phone? Gym in the office? Dedicated parking spot? Day care?
- What kind of salary would make you happy? How about year-end bonus?
- Other details of your compensation package? 401(k) matching? Profit sharing? Stock options?

The list should be as long as necessary to cover all the points of interest to you. Never sell yourself short, but be reasonable. While we all desire a lavish compensation package, consider what is realistic given your current and potential skill sets and opportunities. This record will form your vision for your new role and ensure you track it. Take as much time as you need to outline what is important to you and remember to use the MVP in Appendix 1 as a guide.

Key Principle: Identification of Interests

Here you are beginning to define your ultimate goal. Most people do not actually take the time to identify what is important to them and consequently limit their results. Before you can set your goal, you need to identify and understand the things that bring you utility (or happiness).

It is no accident that salary is one of the last questions on our list. When most people think of negotiating their job offer, salary immediately comes to mind. However, as you are about to see, that dollar amount may not be the most important condition for you. For example, consider the two compensation packages below in Figure 2. Looking beyond just salary, which offer would you rather accept?

If you focus on salary, Offer 1 is clearly more attractive. However, when taking the other factors into account, the first offer may not be as appealing. While many people would opt for the latter option with its perks, very few realize that virtually all of these non-salary benefits are attainable.

Figure 2: If you focus on salary, you'd likely choose Offer 1. Looking at all factors, you'll probably agree Offer 2 is more attractive.		**Offer 1**	**Offer 2**
	Salary	$150,000	$120,000
	Working Hours	90 hours/week	50 hours/week
	Travel	Several days per week	Flexible
	Perks	None	All cell bills paid Free health club Free day care

Most people focus on salary as the primary driver for changing jobs or beginning a new career. However, very few people concentrate on (or even ask for) these other—often more easily attained—forms of compensation. Be sure to consider these non-salary aspects and include them in your vision. As you will see shortly, maintaining this "big picture" approach will help ensure that you obtain the best possible outcome when negotiating your compensation.

Visualize

> ### Key Principle: Goal Setting
> You may have heard that people are 3-4 times more likely to accomplish something when they write it down. The simple reason is that putting your thoughts on paper makes them more real in your mind and leads to action. Further refining these thoughts into specific and measurable goals that you regularly review will virtually ensure success. Always know your aim, make it tangible and write it down. You can always revise it, but start immediately. The summation of these goals will comprise your vision for your future job.

Explaining your goals may be as simple as stating, "I would like a job that compensates me with _____, allows me to do _____, challenges me by _____ and offers the promotion opportunity to do _____." The content of this sentence is up to you.

Using your list of characteristics from above as a guide, draft your vision (which you can always modify) at the bottom of your MVP.

STEP 2: REFINE YOUR VISION

Next, return to your list of characteristics and rank each one in order of importance. Your MVP is designed to help organize these rankings through the "Importance" columns. Rank each attribute from 1 to 3, with a 1 reserved for items that are "deal breakers," meaning they are so important that you cannot accept the job without them. 2's will be major points in your compensation package, while a 3 represents something nice to have, but not necessarily that important to you. If you find your list of key attributes (1's and 2's) is long, note up to 5 or 6 that are most important to you.

Key Principle: Prioritizing Interests

All of the above items, particularly the deal breakers, are of significant interest. Here you are beginning to establish what really matters to you. Listing these points in order of priority will give you the proper perspective when negotiating. Having written down your goals, you are prioritizing the interests that will help you attain the outcome you desire—in this case, great compensation!

Before moving to the second stage, Analysis, take another look at your vision as stated at the bottom of your MVP. Does it capture your key prioritized interests? Update and refine your vision if necessary. It may be helpful to read Step 1 again now that you have confirmed which interests are most important. Take as much time as you need to come up with a vision/goal that not only feels comfortable, but excites you.

Stage Two

Analyze Your Situation

Now that we know your goals and vision, we will examine how closely they align with your current situation. We will evaluate and compare your new (or prospective) job opportunities and your current position. This comparison leads to an analysis of the company (or companies) offering you employment. Successfully completing these four steps sets the stage for your strategy development, where you will form a plan to meet your goals.

STEP 3: NEW (OR PROSPECTIVE) OFFER ANALYSIS

Write down all the details of your new job offer in the next column of the MVP. If you do not currently have a new job offer, you can move ahead to Step 4 or use this space to describe a prospective job opportunity that you are considering.

Use the characteristics listed in Steps 1 and 2 as a guide to list all the important details of this new opportunity, such as location, hours/flexibility, salary, bonus, etc. Of course, if your new offer identifies additional key characteristics not already noted, be sure to add them to the list.

STEP 4: CURRENT JOB ANALYSIS

Use the next column of the MVP to describe all aspects of your current job. If you are not currently employed, you may reference your most recent job or simply proceed to Step 5 to compare your ideal position with the one(s) offered to you.

STEP 5: COMPARATIVE ANALYSIS

Now, step back and review your completed MVP. Pay close attention to how your prioritized list of job characteristics compares to the lists created in Steps 3 and 4. How many of these key items appear in your new job? How about in your current job? Identifying what is most important to you, is one opportunity clearly a better fit than the other? These are the right questions to begin thinking about at this stage. This analysis will help you weigh your new opportunity against your existing one.

This exercise's importance lies in its ability to clearly illustrate each option's benefits. We recommend you complete this analysis every 6-12 months, regardless of whether or not you are actively seeking new employment. Doing so will ensure your current job and your goals are in sync at all times.

From this moment forward, we will assume you wish to pursue the new opportunity. However, should you choose to remain at your current job or are still undecided, you can use the following steps and principles in other ways. For example, should you feel that your current job is not helping you meet enough of your key goals, these exercises will help you negotiate with your existing employer to improve your situation. Similarly, it will allow you to compare your current situation with other opportunities that may be available to you.

STEP 6: COUNTERPART ANALYSIS

Your next step is to evaluate the other party. Successful preparation requires looking at the following three elements:

A. Motivation: Identify and analyze the interests of the company that made the offer.
B. Reasoning: Assess the company's rationale for this specific compensation package.
C. Representation: Evaluate the individuals with whom you will directly interact in the job offer negotiation process.

As you consider each of these three components and the questions listed below, you can use the Counterpart Analysis Plan (CAP) in Appendix 2 to record your key thoughts and observations.

Part A - Motivation: The goal here is to understand more about the company's interest in you. Let's focus on the larger picture and explore what is driving the company's proposed compensation package. Important questions to contemplate include:

- What are the specific reasons this company is making you an offer?
- What does the company hope to accomplish? What role does it want you to fill? Of course the company wants to hire you (congratulations!), but why?
- How soon do they want you to start work? Urgency may signal an immediate need and more room to negotiate terms.
- Is it a rapidly growing firm?
- What specific parts of your personality led to the offer? Do you have some unique expertise or specialty the company desires?
- Have the representatives expressed how anxious they are to hire you?

Part B - Reasoning: Now, we'll examine the factors that drove the company to offer you the detailed compensation package. Important questions to consider here include:

- Are the salary and compensation package above, below or at the industry average?
- Based on size and financial position, what does the company see as most important?
  - Is it a tiny startup firm that is strapped for cash? In this case, salary may not be negotiable, but incentive-based bonuses, profit sharing or stock options may be available instead.
  - Is it a large company that makes similar offers to dozens of people in your position? In this case, the company may have rules or policies stating a salary cannot be increased beyond an existing level. However, you may be able to obtain a larger sign-on bonus, an extra week of vacation, or reimbursement for your cell phone and gas bills, among other potential perks.

Analyze

▸ Do your new managers want you to start right away? Or perhaps they want you to consider traveling quite a bit. Maybe they just really value you and want to get you to accept the offer. As a result, they may be willing to offer you more vacation days or potentially pay you a higher salary, as examples. To explore the possibilities, you just need to know how to ask.

Part C - Representation: Next, you will assess the Individual Counterparty or Counterparties. Within all of these interactions lies extremely valuable information that you may be able to use as leverage. Questions to consider include:

▸ To date, with whom have you interacted at the company? Are these individuals from the division in which you will work and/or from the Human Resources (HR) Department?

▸ What specific comments have they made to you regarding why they wish to hire you or what they like about you?

▸ Have they made any comments that indicate how urgently they want to hire you? Or why this is the case?

▸ Have they commented about roles they'd like you to take on that go beyond the responsibilities of the role for which you have applied?

▸ Have you met your potential supervisor or co-workers? What have they told you? What are their individual goals in hiring you? Specifically, what will they accomplish by hiring you? Do they need help getting their jobs done? Do they need you to manage an important initiative that will help them?

▸ From a Human Resources standpoint, what do they have to gain by hiring you? For example, they may have interviewed dozens of candidates and only liked you. Should you accept the offer, they would be done with the process, leaving them one less task.

In answering the above questions, you've put yourself in the company's position. Gaining perspective on the representatives' motivation enables you to create an ideal strategy that best meets your needs, as well as those of the company.

Key Principle: Identifying Other Party Interests

Understanding the other party's motives, interests and goals is a critical part of preparing for your negotiation, as it helps you determine the appropriate strategy. It may also identify opportunities for mutual benefit that will put you and the other party in a better position. Remember that very few negotiations are exclusively a "zero sum game" whereby a gain by one party necessitates a loss by the other. Quite often, you'll be able to create situations where both parties can benefit.

With your MVP and CAP complete, you are now halfway there. Next, we'll move on to developing the strategy that will help you obtain the goals you seek.

Stage Three

Assemble Your Strategy

Now that you have analyzed your interests and those of the company with which you are negotiating, you are ready to formulate your negotiation strategy. In this stage, we will introduce you to numerous tools and techniques that you will use to optimize your negotiations and best position yourself to obtain the outcome that you desire.

STEP 7: BEGIN FORMING YOUR STRATEGY

Armed with a better understanding of your counterparty, let's refer again to your MVP and the Comparative Analysis you completed in Step 5. Paying close attention to the characteristics ranked as 1's and 2's on your MVP, review how many items the new company offers. The analysis you accomplished in Step 6 (CAP worksheet) should help you understand what drove the company to offer or not offer these particular benefits.

From your own research, experience and gut feel, you may believe you have a strong sense of what you can and cannot obtain from the company. However, don't write anything off just yet. Remember, you won't get something unless you ask for it. Think about what you truly want and pursue those things, whether large or small. Once you have identified these items, you've already begun to formulate a strategy.

As we begin, refer now to the Strategy Formulation Worksheet in Appendix 3, which will guide you through the process of recording and perfecting your negotiation strategy.

Strategy Sub-Steps 1-2: Strategy Formulation
1. Examine Prioritized List of Goals (*Key Principles: Prioritizing Interests, Preparation*)

Strategize

2. Review Comparative Analysis: What items are they not offering to you? Pay particular attention to deal breakers and items of major importance. (*Key Principle: Preparation*)

> **Key Principle: Preparation**
>
> The most effective negotiations are based on solid preparation. As we have emphasized, you should know your goals and interests, understand the other party's goals and interests, identify and understand any relevant third party information, and prepare a strategy based on what you have learned. Completing these steps will ensure you are as prepared as possible for your upcoming negotiations.

With your prioritized list and CAP analysis finalized, you are ready to optimize the strategy you will use to achieve your goals.

STEP 8: STRATEGY OPTIMIZATION – LEVERAGING KEY TOOLS

Now that you understand what you want to obtain and have done a good deal of preparation, we will introduce you to several key principles you can use to optimize your negotiation strategy.

Strategy Sub-Steps 3-8: Strategy Optimization

3. Identify Deficiencies in Their Offer: How can you obtain these missing items? Look at each compensation area one by one.

   a. Industry/Competitive Analysis: Does a similar company or position offer this compensation component? (*Key Principles: Leveraging External Information/Relationships, Situational Norms*)

Key Principle: Leveraging External Information/Relationships

External factors can guide a negotiation in a positive direction. Information about your circumstances, such as a job offer from a competitor or general industry information (related to salary, vacation, etc.) can be used as a reference point when it aligns with your vision. Relationships can be even more valuable. Sharing a common friend or business relationship with the other party can add credibility, as well as aid from a facilitator standpoint.

Key Principle: Situational Norms

Situational norms are defined as a company's practice or policy that legitimizes a decision. This is a concept with which we are all familiar. For example, how many times have you heard someone say "I'm sorry, but we can't do that because it's against store policy" or "Our policy on _____ is _____." Many people hide behind policy or use it as a reference point. While such situational norms can seem intimidating on the surface, you can actually use them to your advantage in a negotiation.

For example, if company representatives tell you they cannot pay you more than $50k because that is their "policy" or that you are in a certain "band level" and are already at the maximum, you can ask questions such as "Have you ever paid anyone more than their band level indicated?" or "Have you ever made an exception to this policy?" "Ever" is a long time, and chances are that they probably have made an exception at some point. People absolutely hate to contradict themselves. Therefore, if they have made an exception, and answer "yes" to a "Have you ever…" question, you've just opened the door to gaining another exception. As it is human nature to want to act in a somewhat consistent manner, you may be able to obtain a similar exception.

b. Relevant Offers Made By This Company: Are any of the items you seek evident in a compensation package that this company offered to individuals in a similar position? (*Key Principles: Leveraging External Information / Relationships, Situational Norms*)

c. Examine the Company "Toolbox": To your knowledge, has the company ever offered this form of compensation? For example, do they have stock options? Do they give sign-on bonuses? While the answer may be no, that does not mean you cannot be the first person to receive a sign-on or relocation bonus. (*Key Principle: Situational Norms*)

d. Unwanted Items: Are they offering any items that are not as important to you? You may be able to trade them for something that is more valuable to you. (*Key Principle: Leveraging Value Gaps*)

Key Principle: Leveraging Value Gaps

The gist of this principle, which can be used in all aspects of daily life, is that there are things you may value more or less than the party with whom you negotiate. While a company may not be able to offer you an increase in salary above an existing level, it is of minimal or no cost to the company to let you work from home on alternating Fridays. However, this opportunity to work from home may give you tremendous utility. Perhaps your company can offer discounts on products it sells or has a service it can offer you.

Imagine you are a salesperson and want to make $100k next year. You expect a base salary of $70k with $30k bonus for reaching your sales quota, but the employer offers $50k with $30k bonus. Without asking key questions, you may walk away. However, you learn that the company is willing to pay additional bonuses of $10k for every 10% by which you exceed your quota. You're convinced you can exceed it by 20% and thus are on your way to making $100k or more. Here, managers value base salary a great deal and are inflexible on fixed costs. However, they also place tremendous value on sales and will reward you when you exceed their goals. You value compensation and are confident in your ability to exceed these goals. By considering such options, you create value for both parties and "enlarge the pie."

4. Re-Prioritization of Your List of Goals: Now that you have a better feel for what is attainable and reasonable, re-prioritize your list. (*Key Principle: Process*)

Key Principle: Process

One of the most important steps in preparing for a negotiation is the creation of a process. Here, it is important to write down and/or clearly articulate the agenda for the negotiation. What are the key points that you want to discuss and in what order? Typically, people begin with items that are most important to them, but it may help to begin with an area of mutual interest, perhaps where it appears you can "enlarge the pie." Many people have found success by intertwining items of high and low priority throughout the negotiation. Here, you want to make sure to address one item at a time. Note that you can always re-examine items at the end of the negotiation and re-open certain ones for discussion.

Strategize

At the end of the day, a process will ensure that you cover all of the points that are important to you. It is very easy to get sidetracked in a negotiation, especially if emotions are heightened. A process will keep you focused on the important issues.

5. Speak to the Right Person: Find the person who actually makes the decisions. Leverage existing relationships within the business—you may need to go beyond HR personnel. (*Key Principle: Find the Decision Maker*)

Key Principle: Find the Decision Maker

In the context of any negotiation, you may be dealing with several parties. To obtain your goals, it is important to speak with the decision maker. That said, you never want to seem impolite or appear to sidestep anyone on the way to the decision maker. Be sure to treat everyone with respect, as you never know who has input into a negotiation, regardless of whether or not they are a direct part of the process.

One point to bear in mind in the context of job offer negotiations: You will often communicate with individuals within the HR department. While the HR rep may appear to hold decision-making power, a business head may be responsible for making the true hiring and compensation decisions, with the HR employee serving as a facilitator.

6. Look for Common Interests: Identify goals and interests that you and your prospective employer share. (*Key Principle: Common Interests*)

Key Principle: Common Interests

It can be to your benefit to point out common interests that you share with the other party. For example, it may be in the interest of both parties that you have a long career with a company. You likely desire a successful career with advancement opportunities, while your employer will wish to benefit from your increasing productivity. Given that you share the same goals, seeking long-term compensation, such as stock options and/or performance bonuses, would seem very attainable.

7. Be Forthright: Remember to be honest and let the other individual(s) know why you are asking for particular points. Feel free to explain the details of your situation, if appropriate. Communicate openly, but also be empathetic to their perspective and rationale for what they can and cannot do. (*Key Principles: Help Them Help You, Humanize Yourself*)

Key Principle: Help Them Help You

In a job offer negotiation, you may face major constraints, including those "deal breakers" you named in Steps 1 and 2. One tool you can use to help obtain these goals is sharing your concerns with the other party and asking their advice on how they can help you handle the situation. The underlying idea is simple: people enjoy helping others. By sharing your concerns, you put the other party in a position of power. The other party in turn feels in control and empowered to help you. This tool creates a positive experience and "humanizes" the situation, making it more personal and less transactional.

Key Principle: Humanize Yourself

Similar to the previous principle, this idea emphasizes the value of appearing as a person, not a transactional entity. In any negotiation, it is important to show that you possess positive core traits, such as empathy. Begin with some small talk and try to find a common interest—even if unrelated to the job or company. The goal is to get the other party to think of your personal traits, not just your job description, when making decisions. Building this rapport is also the first step to a lasting relationship with the other party, leading to a more positive work environment and aiding future negotiations.

8. Collaboration is Key: The goal in any negotiation is to make it a collaborative effort. Work with the other party to mutually settle on what you want. Feel free to use other key principles, such as ties, if they are relevant. You'll get there and once you do, congratulations!

Key Principle: Ties

A vast majority of negotiations revolve around long-term relationships. Whether you are dealing with a company, family, friends or a storekeeper, chances are you are going to interact (or negotiate) with these parties more than once. In each of these cases, one tool always at your fingertips is using ties. You can tie an existing negotiation to a future one. Imagine negotiating with a storeowner when you seek a discounted price on an item. You may promise to shop there more often or to refer a friend or two. Another example of tying would be asking for a discount on a future item or purchase, if you cannot obtain a discount at this time.

In the context of a job offer, you can link something short term, such as your salary or sign-on bonus, to something longer term, such as a promise to take on a new responsibility at a future date, refer a colleague or help bring in some new business to the company if you are hired.

Note of caution: It is important to never make empty promises. While such promises may allow you to get what you want in the short term, they may come back to harm you. Remember that all negotiations are part of broader long-lasting relationships.

Strategy - Final Thoughts:

Above all, remember the importance of collaboration and fairness in the negotiation process. Unless you are convinced your audience will receive it well, don't be too aggressive or appear overly competitive. You are building a relationship and if you choose to work for this company, this negotiation is the first of many you will conduct throughout your career. Remember, you are negotiating with people, not an entity. The goal is for all people involved to walk away happy.

When you negotiate effectively, the negotiation will be integrative—that is, both parties will be better off than they were before, creating more total value or utility. Value and utility include both tangible items (salary, bonus, vacation, company car, etc.) and intangible items (self-actualization, responsibility, a great working relationship, positive feelings, etc.). The goal here is to effectively "enlarge the pie" that you have to share. Less than ideal negotiations tend to be more distributive—both parties view the total value or utility as a fixed amount and aim to get as much of it as possible. These negotiations tend to be more adversarial and ignore the tools we set out for you. Rather than focus on how to "split the pie," use these tools to help ensure that your negotiations are integrative and result in optimal outcomes for all parties involved.

Stage Four

Implement Your Strategy

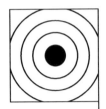

Now that you have a strategy, have prepared for the negotiation and have a process in place, you're ready to begin negotiating. If you have the luxury of time and resources, we strongly recommend that you practice. Once you feel comfortable with your process, it will be time to move forward with the actual negotiation.

STEP 9: PRACTICE TO PERFECTION

Like everything else in life, the more you practice, the better you will be. Before speaking to the company, practice implementing your strategy through a mock session with a trusted friend or family member. This step is your opportunity to perfect your approach before the big day. Just as preparation puts you in the best position for a job interview or exam, practicing this conversation will ease your nerves and hone your technique.

A thorough review of this session is invaluable as well. You may even wish to tape it, to support your analysis. Consider how your strategy worked in action—did the techniques you chose aid the discussion? Did the conversation feel collaborative yet allow you to achieve your goals? To evaluate your exchange, think of how you would feel meeting this person again after the interaction you shared. Other key points to consider include your body language, rapport, appearance and of course, results.

STEP 10: NEGOTIATE!

Having completed the preceding steps, you're now ready to begin. With these new principles in mind, use the vision and strategy you developed to negotiate the points you desire. You can also leverage the Glossary of Key Negotiating Principles, which offers short summaries of each key principle.

You now have all of the tools necessary to become an extremely effective negotiator. Best of luck!

Implement

Should you seek expert guidance on any specific negotiation or desire broader negotiations coaching, please visit us at www.1-hourexpert.com. We look forward to continuing to help you become the best negotiator possible.

We are also very interested in hearing your success stories. Please let us know the results of your job offer negotiations by e-mailing us at info@1-hourexpert.com.

Glossary of Key Negotiating Principles

Common Interests
Look for interests that both parties share. Use this common ground to reach your goal. (page 21)

Find the Decision Maker
Make sure you are speaking with the individual who can take action on your requests and has the power to make the decisions. Show respect to all parties, even if they are not decision makers. (page 20)

Goal Setting
Given your interests, what are your goals? What is your ideal scenario? (page 6)

Help Them Help You
Communicate your concerns. Put other parties in a position of power so they can help you. (page 21)

Humanize Yourself
Make yourself a human being, not a "negotiating entity." Find a way to relate to the other side. Personalize the interaction to obtain optimal results. (page 22)

Identification of Interests
What are your interests? What do you want to obtain? (page 4)

Identifying Other Party Interests
Put yourself in their shoes. What are their interests? Look beyond what they are saying and understand why they are saying it. (page 13)

Leveraging External Information / Relationships
Seek out all relevant third party information, such as competitor or industry compensation, comparable job offers and common relationships you share with the other party. (page 17)

Leveraging Value Gaps
Look for items that are of more value to one of the parties. Trade what is more important to the other side for something that is more valuable to you. (page 18)

Preparation
Know as much as you can about yourself, the other party and relevant external information. Follow the 10 steps to ensure you are prepared! (page 16)

Glossary (cont'd)

Prioritizing Interests

Which of your interests are most important to you? Which are not as important? (page 7)

Process

Set up a process as a guide to your negotiation to ensure that you do not forget to address any points. Processes also help you remain objective. (page 19)

Situational Norms

Look for any norms or standards that the party has or may use. Look for exceptions to any norms, if possible. Reposition your goals within their norms. (page 17)

Ties

Tie this negotiation to future negotiations if possible. Keep your eye on the relationship, as that is most important. No empty promises. (page 22)

Appendix 1: Master Vision Preparation (MVP) Worksheet (Steps 1-5, pages 3-10)

Characteristic	Ideal Job	New Job	Current Job	Importance		
				1 Deal Breaker	2 Major	3 Moderate
Role/Position						
Key Responsibilities						
Advancement Opportunities/ Timeline						
Office Specifics						
Location						
Travel Requirements						
Working Hours/ Schedule						
Supervisor/ Management						
Supervisee(s)						

Appendix 1: Master Vision Preparation (MVP) Worksheet (Steps 1-5) cont'd

Characteristic	Ideal Job	New Job	Current Job	Importance 1 Deal Breaker	Importance 2 Major	Importance 3 Moderate
Vacation						
Medical Benefits						
Other Benefits Company Car? Cell Phone? Gym? Parking? Day Care?						
Salary/Bonus						
401k						
Profit Sharing/ Options						

Vision: _____

_____

_____

Appendix 1B: (Template) Master Vision Preparation (MVP) Worksheet (Steps 1-5, pages 3-10)

Characteristic	Ideal Job	New Job	Current Job	Importance		
				1 Deal Breaker	2 Major	3 Moderate

Appendix 1B: (Template) Master Vision Preparation (MVP) Worksheet (Steps 1-5) cont'd

Characteristic	Ideal Job	New Job	Current Job	Importance 1 Deal Breaker	Importance 2 Major	Importance 3 Moderate

Vision: _____

_____

_____

Appendix 2: Counterpart Analysis Plan (CAP) Worksheet (Step 6, pages 10-13)

Motivation

Identify and analyze the interests of the company that made the offer.

Reasoning

Assess the company's rationale for this specific compensation package.

Representation

Evaluate the individuals with whom you will directly interact.

Appendix 3: Strategy Formulation (SF) Worksheet (Steps 7-8, pages 15-23)

1. Review Prioritized Set of Goals		4. Re-Prioritization of Your List of Goals
2. Review Comparative Analysis		5. Speak to the Right Person
3. Identify Deficiencies in Their Offer		6. Look for Common Interests
a. Industry/ Competitive Analysis		7. Be Forthright
b. Relevant Offers		8. Collaboration is Key
c. The Company "Toolbox"		Other Notes
d. Unwanted Items		

Made in the USA
Lexington, KY
23 February 2010